NO SEW,
NO PROBLEM

Snap books®

No-Sew
DRESSES, SKIRTS,
AND OTHER CLOTHING

by Karen Latchana Kenney

CAPSTONE PRESS
a capstone imprint

Snap Books are published by Capstone Press, 1710 Roe Crest Drive,
North Mankato, Minnesota 56003
www.mycapstone.com

Library of Congress Cataloging-in-Publication Data
Names: Kenney, Karen Latchana, author.
Title: No-sew dresses, skirts, and other clothing / by Karen Latchana Kenney.
Description: North Mankato, Minnesota : Capstone Press, [2019] | Series: Snap
    books. No sew, no problem | Audience: Age 9-14.
Identifiers: LCCN 2018010998 (print) | LCCN 2018023545 (ebook) |
    ISBN 9781543525595 (eBook PDF) |
    ISBN 9781543525519 (library binding)
Subjects: LCSH: Textile crafts—Juvenile literature. | Dressmaking—Juvenile
    literature. | Clothing and dress—Juvenile literature.
Classification: LCC TT699 (ebook) | LCC TT699 .K459 2019 (print) | DDC
    646.4—dc23
LC record available at https://lccn.loc.gov/2018010998

Editorial Credits
Abby Colich, editor; Kayla Rossow, designer; Jo Miller, photo researcher;
Laura Manthe, production specialist

Image Credits
All photographs by Capstone Studio: TJ Thoraldson Digital Photography, Craft Product
Producers: All done by Jennifer Reeb

Design Elements: Capstone and Shutterstock

Table of Contents

Not Sewing Is So Easy

Are you bored with the same old wardrobe? Do you want to make your own clothes but don't know how to sew? Or maybe you just don't have time? Whether you're a crafty pro or still learning the basics, there are plenty of clothes you can make. Give some of your old clothes a new makeover. Or make new clothes from just a few pieces of fabric. Then add your own style. You don't have to follow the instructions exactly. Experiment with different embellishments or designs. Create looks that are all your own.

Tip

Make sure an adult is nearby to help when using an iron, hot glue, or sharp knives.

Fabric and Glue How-To

You can reuse or upcycle old pieces of fabric or clothing. Fabric from a store comes on a bolt or roll. The fabric width is predetermined. You will choose the length. Make sure you read through the project ahead of time and take any necessary measurements before buying fabric.

For some projects, you'll just need to cut a piece of fabric to size. Others, however, will need glue or adhesive to hold pieces of fabric together. A hot glue gun works great for heavier pieces. More lightweight clothing uses fabric glue. Be sure you buy a glue that is labeled permanent, washable, and flexible. Fusible bonding tape also works well to create hems and seams. It uses the heat from an iron to bond fabric together. Be sure to follow the instructions on the package.

Caring for Your Clothes

Fabric glue and fusible tape work great to make hems or connect pieces of fabric. Glued and fused fabrics will last, but only with the right care. Painted areas need some special care too. Turn your clothing inside out to protect painted designs. Hand wash your clothing, using a gentle fabric detergent. Be sure to hang-dry your creations. Do not put them in the dryer.

Simple Summer Dress

On hot summer days, dresses are your go-to fashion statement.
Turn a maxi skirt into your newest breezy summer dress.
Use an old skirt or find one at a thrift store. Keep it simple
or add some stripes, dye, or studs to dress it up.

What You'll Need

- maxi skirt (one size larger than your normal size)
- scissors
- fusible tape
- iron and ironing board
- fabric ribbon
- measuring tape
- fabric glue
- eyelets and eyelet tool

What You'll Do

1. Cut the waistband off the maxi skirt, keeping it in one piece. You'll use it to make a belt later.

2. Cut 8 inches (20.3 cm) down from the top along both side seams. These will be the armholes.

3. At the bottom of each cut, make a T-shape by cutting a 0.5-inch (1.3-cm) slit in each direction.

4. Turn the skirt inside out. Fold in the sides of the armholes. Following the package instructions, use fusible tape and an iron to bond the folded sides to the fabric.

5. Cut two pieces of ribbon, each the length of the skirt's cut top plus 16 inches (40.6 cm).

6. Lay one ribbon along one top side of the skirt. Fold the top down to cover the ribbon. Use fusible tape and an iron to secure the bottom of the flap to the inside of the skirt, leaving a pocket for the ribbon to move freely. Make sure the fusible tape does not touch the ribbon.

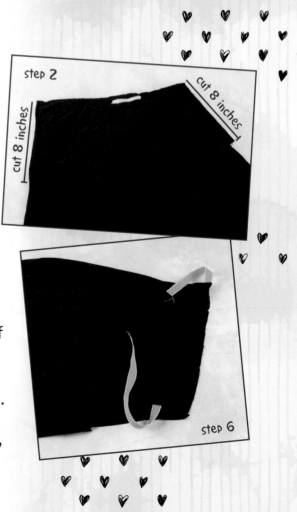

step 2

cut 8 inches

cut 8 inches

step 6

7. Repeat step 6 for the other side of the skirt and the other ribbon. Turn the skirt right side out. Tie the ribbons together on each side of the skirt to create the straps of the dress.

8. Now make a belt from the waistband. Pull the waistband over your waist to check for size. If needed, cut it to fit plus 2 inches (5.1 cm). Fold in the edges 0.5 inch (1.3 cm) and glue down with fabric glue to create a hem.

9. Use the eyelet tool to add an eyelet next to each hem in the center of the belt. Cut an 8-inch (20.3-cm) piece of ribbon. Thread the ribbon through each eyelet and tie in a bow.

10. Now put on your dress! Adjust the shoulder straps and belt until the dress fits you correctly.

step 9

Dress Up Your Dress!

Try these tricks to make your dress a little dressier:

× Make colorful stripes by the neckline or the bottom hem with iron-on trim tape.

× Attach pyramid or round studs around the neckline or bottom hem.

× Bleach-dye a pattern onto the skirt before you cut it. Stick a piece of cardboard between the layers and lay the skirt outside. Use painter's tape to create shapes or stripes. Be sure to do both sides. Fill a spray bottle with a half-and-half mix of bleach and water. Spray your skirt all over on both sides. Let it sit for 5 to 10 minutes until it is as light as you want it to be. Then remove the tape and rinse your skirt in cold water.

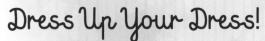

Studded Necklace T-shirt

You're meeting up with some friends. The only thing in your closet is a boring T-shirt, but you want to look a little more fun. Glam up that plain top with just a few cuts, studs, and ribbon. You won't even need to wear jewelry with this shirt!

What You'll Need

- crew neck T-shirt
- cardboard
- chalk
- scissors
- ribbon
- fabric studs

What You'll Do

1. Slip the cardboard inside the T-shirt. Lay on your work area with the front of the shirt facing up.

2. With the chalk, draw four semicircles about 0.25 inch (0.6 cm) apart along the neckline. They should curve like a necklace.

3. Cut along the lines to make loose strips. Cut out the lowest strip and discard.

4. Measure a length of ribbon by laying it along one of the loose strips of the shirt. Cut it about 1 inch (2.5 cm) longer than the strip.

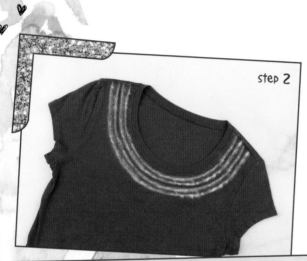
step 2

step 3

5. Grab two of the cut strips at the end where they meet the rest of the T-shirt. Tie one end of the ribbon around them. Attach a stud around the knot.

6. Tie the other end of the ribbon at the other end of the strips. Attach a stud around the knot.

7. Repeat steps 5 and 6 for the remaining strips to make a pretty necklace neckline.

step 5

Tip
Gently pull on the T-shirt strips to stretch and curl them.

Two-Tone Tulle Skirt

Need something fancy for Friday night's party?
Try making this light and full tulle skirt.
It's simple to make, but will look like it came
from a designer store. You'll feel like
royalty the minute you try it on.

What You'll Need

- crochet headband stretch trim, 1.75 inches (4.4 cm) wide
- scissors
- cardboard
- 4 spools of tulle in two colors

What You'll Do

1. Wrap the headband trim once around your waist. Add 4 inches (10.2 cm) and cut a piece to this length. Tie the piece around your waist and make a knot. Then take it off and put it around the cardboard.

2. Measure a length of tulle by holding one end to your waist. Unroll the spool until it reaches where you want the skirt to end. Then double the piece of tulle and cut it. Cut around 10 strips of this length in one color. Cut 10 strips an inch or two shorter in the other color. You can cut more later if you need a fuller skirt.

3. Fold one piece of tulle in half. Place the folded end under the headband trim and push through hole in the second to bottom row. Pull the loop through the front side of the trim about 2 inches (5.1 cm).

step 2

step 3

4. Pull the cut ends of the tulle up through the loop and pull down tightly. Repeat, evenly spacing the tulle to make one complete row.

5. Repeats steps 3 to 5 with the other color to make a second row of tulle using the above row of holes on the trim. Fill in with more tulle if needed.

Sweater Coat

When a chill is in the air, you need just the right top to keep warm. A cozy sweater coat is perfect for a fall day. Pick a fabric that speaks to you or find a neutral color that goes with several of your outfits.

What You'll Need

- woven sweater fabric, 1 x 2 yards (0.9 x 1.8 m)
- scissors
- dinner plate
- fabric chalk
- measuring tape
- hot glue gun and glue sticks
- belt

What You'll Do

1. Fold your fabric so the short sides are touching and the fabric is facing right side out. The folded part will sit on your shoulders when the coat is finished.

2. Line up the edges and trim off any fray.

3. Place the plate on top of one of the bottom unfolded corners. Trace the rounded edge of the plate. Repeat on the other side. Cut along the traced line through both layers of fabric to make rounded edges.

4. Find the middle of the fabric's folded edge. Draw a line 6-inches (15.2-cm) straight down from this point. Measure along the top fold 6 inches (15.2 cm) each way from the top center point. Draw lines connecting each of those points to the bottom of the first line, making triangles. Cut out along those lines through only one layer of fabric. This will be your neck hole.

step 3

step 4

5. Measure from the top of your shoulder to your waist. Use the chalk to mark the same distance down the front of the coat from the center of the folded crease.

6. Measure around your waist. Add a few inches and divide in half. Mark this measurement to each side of the mark you just made. Cut a 1.5-inch (3.8-cm) slit at each of these spots through both layers of fabric. These will be your belt holes.

slits for belt (step 6)

7. Turn the fabric inside out. Add a line of hot glue (a few inches at a time) along the edge. Roll the fabric over the glue and press down to create a hem. Let dry completely.

8. Thread a belt through the holes on one side, around the back, and back through the other holes. Now tighten the belt to fit.

Easy Strap Belt

If you don't have a belt to go with your new coat, make a new one. Cut enough nylon strap to fit around your waist plus 6 inches (15.2 cm). Put one end of the strap through two 1.5-inch (3.8-cm) metal D rings. Fold the strap over and glue down to secure the D rings in the loop. Press firmly as the glue dries. Fold over the other end of the strap to create a hem and glue in place. Let dry completely.

Fringed Kimono Wrap

Need some flair for your new summer outfit? Take plain fabric, make your own unique design, and choose a color to dye. You can wear this light kimono all summer long.

What You'll Need

- white lightweight fabric with white dye resistant stitching, 41 x 60 inches (104.1 x 152.4 cm)
- fabric dye
- measuring tape
- pins
- 2 yards (1.8 m) fringe trim
- 50 fabric studs
- scissors

What You'll Do

1. Following package directions, dye your fabric. When finished, wash the fabric. Let dry completely.
2. Fold the fabric so the long edges line up. Lay it flat on your work surface. Find the middle of the fabric. Measure 15 inches (38.1 cm) in each direction. Mark each spot with a pin.
3. To add the fringe, line it up along the long edge of the pinned fabric from one end to the other.

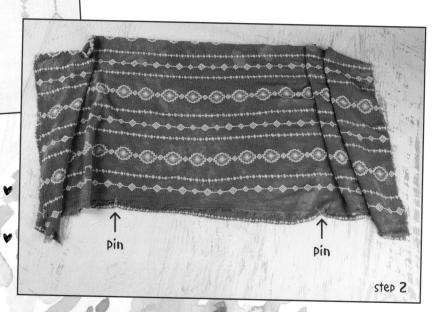

pin   pin

step 2

4. Starting at one end, push a stud through the fringe and through both layers of fabric. Once you reach the first pin, only push the studs through one layer of fabric until you reach the next pin. Then continue pushing the studs through both layers of fabric. Flatten the studs on the back of each prong. Trim off any extra fringe.

step 4

Tip
Make sure all points of the studs make it through the fabric and the fringe.

Mini Caftan Dress

This caftan dress may look simple, but it's a versatile addition to any wardrobe. Wear it with shorts, leggings, or over a bathing suit. It's easy to make and comfy too.

What You'll Need

- solid or patterned thin cotton fabric, 1.5 x 2 yards (1.4 x 1.8 m)
- scissors
- measuring tape
- chalk
- cardboard
- fabric glue
- iron-on trim or ribbon

What You'll Do

1. Fold the fabric in half with the short sides touching and the right sides facing out.

2. Hold the folded piece of fabric up to your body with the crease running from hand to hand. If you want shorter sleeves, cut some length off from one side of the fabric. Trim off any frayed edges.

3. Lay the fabric flat on your work area. Measure to the middle of the crease of the fold. Start by making a tiny slit at the crease and cut straight down through one layer of fabric about 6 inches (15.2 cm). Then cut 4 inches (10.2 cm) along the fold in each direction from the middle point. Cut off the triangles to make a V-neck shape.

4. Turn the fabric inside out. Draw a line on the inside of the fabric 8 to 12 inches (20.3 to 30.5 cm) in from the edge. Begin at the bottom and stop about 10 inches (25.4 cm) from the top folded edge. Repeat on the other side. Make sure you start the line at the same distance in from the edge as the first side.

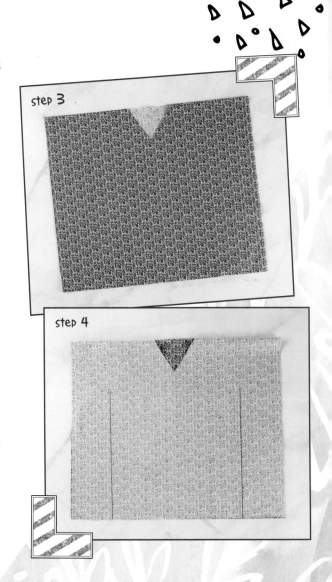

step 3

step 4

5. Turn the fabric right side out. Put cardboard under the dress to protect the surface below it. Use a line of fabric glue to bond the dress at each of those two lines. Make sure the glue is in between the wrong sides of the fabric. Let the glue dry completely.

6. Use iron-on trim or glue ribbon to add a design around the neckline of the dress.

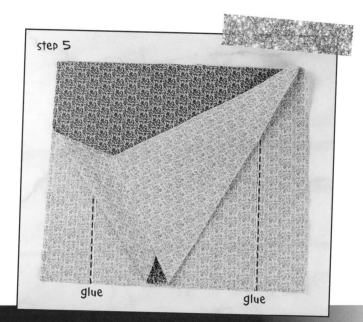

step 5

glue

glue

Tip

To find the correct measurement of the side seams, slip the dress over your head. Pull it against your waist. Make marks on the dress at both sides.

Painted Maxi Dress

This long, flowing maxi dress must be difficult to make, right? Wrong! It's really easy and you don't even have to sew. Use plain fabric and paint on a pattern for your own unique design. Pair this pretty maxi with a big belt to complete your look.

What You'll Need

- solid color lightweight jersey fabric, 1.6 x 2 yards (1.5 x 1.8 m)
- measuring tape
- scissors
- fabric glue
- tarp
- lace or mesh fabric with a pattern
- spray fabric paint

What You'll Do

1. Fold your fabric in half with the long sides touching and the wrong sides facing out.

2. Cut 6 inches (15.2 cm) in from one end along the crease. At the same end, use a line of fabric glue about 0.5 inch (1.3 cm) in from the edge to glue together the short ends of the fabric.

3. Leaving open 6 inches (15.2 cm) from the glued short end, use a line of glue about 0.5 inch (1.3 cm) in from the edge to glue the long ends together. You should have two 6-inch (15.2-cm) armholes on each side. Let dry completely.

4. Measure to the middle point of the glued short end. Make a cut about 6 inches (15.2 cm) down through both layers of fabric. This will be the neckline.

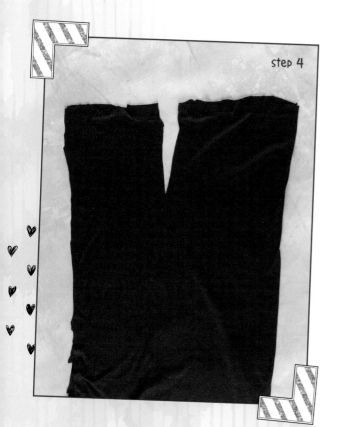
step 4

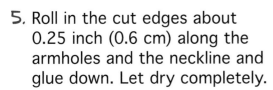

5. Roll in the cut edges about 0.25 inch (0.6 cm) along the armholes and the neckline and glue down. Let dry completely.

6. Turn the dress right side out. Try it on. If it's too long, trim the bottom. Along the bottom edges of the dress, roll the fabric toward the inside of the dress about 0.25 inch (0.6 cm) and glue down to make a hem.

7. Take the dress outside or into a large workspace. Lay it flat on a tarp to protect the surface below.

8. Lay your lace or mesh fabric over the dress. Spray the fabric paint over it. Remove the lace or mesh to see the pattern. Let the paint dry completely before wearing.

STEP 8

Stylish Sweater Skirt

Cold weather isn't always fun. Cold-weather wear isn't always fun either. Bundling up to go outside can get boring, but it doesn't have to be! Turn a thrift store sweater into a sassy new skirt. Then add your own design using the leftover fabric.

What You'll Need

- long sweater
- fabric chalk
- scissors
- hot glue gun and glue sticks
- braided elastic, 0.5 inch (1.3 cm) wide
- safety pin
- felt for flowers, if desired

What You'll Do

1. Mark a straight line with chalk across the sweater from the bottom of one armhole to the other. Then cut through both fabric layers along the line. This edge will form the top of your skirt.

step 1

2. Turn the sweater inside out. Fold the top edge down 1 inch (2.5 cm) to make a hem. Glue all along the edge, leaving a 1-inch (2.5-cm) opening to insert the elastic later. Press the edge down to secure. Let dry completely.

3. Wrap the elastic around your waist. Add a few inches and cut it. Attach a safety pin at one end.

4. Thread the elastic through the 1-inch (2.5-cm) opening from step 2. Use the safety pin to feed it through.

5. Put the skirt on and tie the elastic to fit your waist. Trim the loose ends. Take off the skirt and finish gluing the hem. Add some posies or other decoration to one front bottom corner, if desired.

step 4

Flower Accessories

To make a flower, trace a round object on the extra fabric from your sweater. Cut out the circle. Then cut it in a spiral toward the middle. Roll up the piece, adding dabs of glue as you go, to a create a flower shape. Add green leaves or another colored flower to complement.

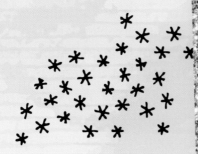

Woven Jersey Skirt

This skirt is comfy, stretchy, and easy to make.
What more could you ask for? Weave in strips of
fabric to make an interesting pattern.
Use different colors for some extra flair.

What You'll Need

- jersey fabric, 1.6 x 2 yards (1.5 x 1.8 m)
- measuring tape and ruler
- scissors
- fabric chalk
- fusible tape
- iron and ironing board
- jersey fabric strips, 1 inch (2.5 cm) wide
- thin fabric strip or ribbon, length of circumference of waist plus 12 inches (30.5 cm)

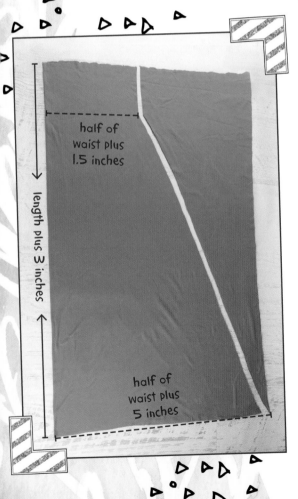

half of waist plus 1.5 inches

length plus 3 inches

half of waist plus 5 inches

What You'll Do

1. Fold fabric in half so that the right sides face one another and the short ends touch. Measure the length you want your skirt to be and add 3 inches (7.6 cm). Measure along the fold and cut off any excess from the bottom through both layers of fabric.

2. Measure around your waist. Take half this measurement and add 1.5 inches (3.8 cm). Measure this length across the top of the fabric beginning at the fold. Draw a line 3 inches (7.6 cm) straight down from this point.

3. Take half your waist measurement and add 5 inches (12.7 cm). Measure this distance along the bottom of the fabric beginning at the fold. Draw a line from your end point to meet the bottom of your first line. Cut along these lines through both layers of fabric.

4. Following the package instructions, use fusible bonding tape to connect the sides you just cut, leaving the top and bottom open. Let cool completely. This seam will be the back of your skirt.

5. Toward one side of the skirt, make tiny horizontal slits stacked in a straight line from top to bottom. Space them 0.5 inch (1.3 cm) apart.

6. Weave a strip of fabric through the holes. Leave 1 inch (2.5 cm) of fabric at the top and glue it down. Leave the other end of the strip hanging out at the bottom of the fabric. Knot it right below the last cut and let the rest of the strip dangle. Repeat to add as many strips as you like.

7. Lay the ribbon or strip for the waistband along the top of the skirt. Fold the top of the skirt over the fabric strip. Following the package instructions, use fusible tape to secure the strip inside of the hem all the way around the skirt. Let cool completely.

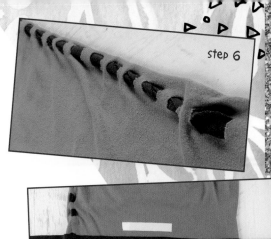

step 6

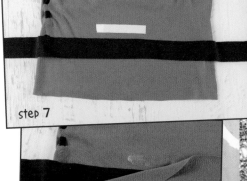

step 7

step 7

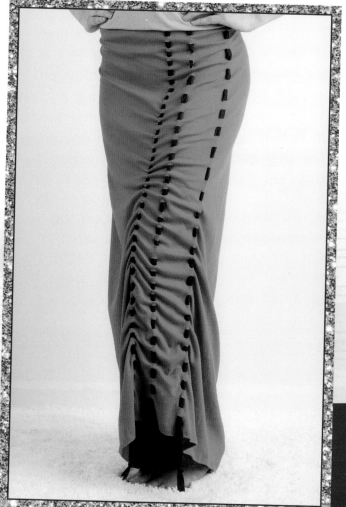

step 8

8. Cut a small slit in the center and pull each end of the waistband through. Tie into a bow to keep the skirt in place around your hips. Turn right side out to wear.

Tip

Cut up an old T-shirt to make strips to weave into your skirt.

23

Tank Dress

For this dress, all you need is a simple tank and some complementing fabric. The empire waist looks great on many different body types. It's your perfect outfit for a summery day.

What You'll Need

- patterned lightweight cotton fabric, 1 yard (0.9 m) wide
- measuring tape
- scissors
- fabric glue
- cotton tank top
- fabric chalk

What You'll Do

1. Wrap the fabric around your waist. Cut it about 4 inches (10.2 cm) longer than your waist. Check the length. Cut the fabric to 2 inches (5.1 cm) longer than your desired length.

2. With the wrong side facing you, fold the bottom edge of the fabric in 1 inch (2.5 cm). Add a line of glue and press down. Let dry.

3. Fold the fabric so the short edges touch and wrong side faces out. Add a line of glue down one edge. Press the two edges together to make a seam. Let dry completely.

4. Try on the tank top and the skirt. Decide where you want the tank to end and the skirt to begin. Add 1 inch (2.5 cm) to the tank and mark with fabric chalk. Remove tank. Use a tape measure or ruler to trace and cut a straight line where you marked your tank to end.

5. Make sure the skirt and the tank top are both wrong side out. Line up the raw edge of the tank top with the top raw edge of the skirt. Make sure the skirt seam falls at the center of the back side of the tank top. Add a line of glue around the bottom of the tank top. Press against the top of the skirt to create a hem. Let dry completely. Turn right side out to wear. Wrap a belt around the waist if desired.

Tip

Press the fabric together tightly after you glue. This helps the glue bond the fabric together.

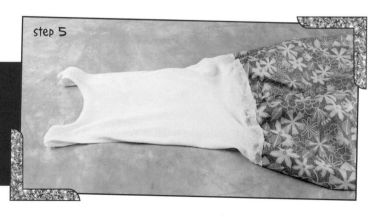

step 5

Cascading Vest

Need something to keep you warm that will look fashionable too? This woolly vest is *so easy* to make—it doesn't even have any hems! The grommet and ribbon edging adds a colorful modern vibe.

What You'll Need

- wool felt fabric, 1 x 1 yard (0.9 x 0.9 m)
- string, about 16 inches (40.6 cm) long
- fabric chalk
- scissors
- measuring tape
- oval pattern
- grommet tool
- grommets
- ribbon (no thicker than the width of the grommet hole)

step 2

step 4

What You'll Do

1. Fold the fabric and then fold it again to get a square with two folded edges and two raw edges.

2. Tie the string to the chalk. Hold one end of the string tightly at the corner of the folded edges. Move the chalk to draw a curved edge along the raw sides. Cut along the curved line.

3. Unfold the fabric. You should have a circle. Fold it so that you have a half circle. Measure the width of your back from shoulder to shoulder.

4. Make a small mark 10 inches (25.4 cm) down from the top of the on the crease. Divide your shoulder to shoulder measurement in half. Measure and mark the distance in a straight line out from the center point you just marked. Flip over your circle and repeat on the other side.

5. From those points, trace the oval pattern to create holes big enough for your arms. Cut out the ovals.

6. Measure and make a mark every inch (2.5 cm) all along the entire edge of the fabric, about 0.25 to 0.5 inch (0.6 to 1.3 cm) from the edge. Use the grommet tool to add grommets at each mark.

7. Now weave ribbon in and out of the holes. After going all the way around, tie the loose ends together. Put your vest on, allowing the top to fold down as a collar.

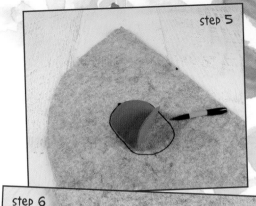
step 5

step 6

Tip

Follow the instructions that come with your grommet tool. Different grommet tools need to be used in different ways.

Precise Cuts

A craft knife may be easier to use than scissors for your grommet holes. They make precise cuts. Cut a small X-shape where the grommet will go. Then press the grommet through. Make sure you have an adult who can help. Craft knives are very sharp. Be sure to use a cutting mat, as they can damage the surface below your fabric.

Striped T-shirt Skirt

With a bit of cutting and some glue, you can turn a plain T-shirt into a casual skirt. Add stripes for a fashion that is all your own. Use a men's T-shirt or a women's T-shirt that is not fitted. A fitted shirt will be too tight for a skirt.

What You'll Need

- solid color T-shirt
- ruler
- fabric chalk
- scissors
- fabric glue

- shoelace
- safety pin
- masking tape
- cardboard
- fabric spray paint

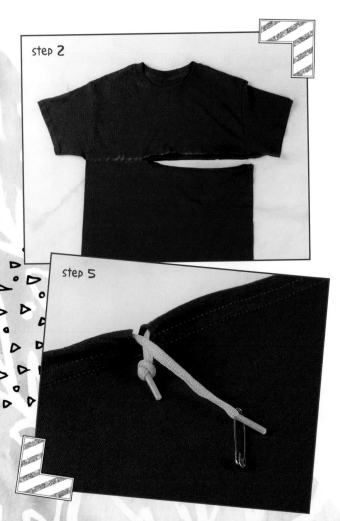

step 2

step 5

What You'll Do

1. Use a ruler to draw a straight line across the T-shirt from the lower end of one armhole to the next.

2. Cut through both layers of the shirt along the line.

3. Turn the shirt inside out. Add a line of glue right at the cut edge. Roll the end over and press down to make a hem. Let dry completely.

4. Turn the shirt back to right side out. Cut a tiny slit in the front center of the bottom hem of the T-shirt.

5. Attach the safety pin to the shoelace. Feed it through the hole you just cut in the hem. Push it all the way around the hem. The two ends of the shoelace should be hanging out of the hole. Flip the shirt around so the string is now at the top.

step 6

6. Lay the skirt flat on your work surface. Stick strips of tape on to make a striped design. Use a ruler to evenly space the stripes.

7. Take the T-shirt outside or place it on a protected surface. Put some cardboard inside the shirt. Then spray paint over your taped design. You may need to add a few coats to get the color you want. Let the paint dry completely. Then peel off the tape.

Tip

Try using a few colors of fabric spray paint instead of just one. You can even go for a splattered paint effect by doing uneven coats. Get creative with your design!

Pretty Painted Cardi

Are you tired of wearing your old sweater?
Don't get rid of it! Turn it into a cardigan. Use a
stencil to create a design and it will feel brand new!

What You'll Need

- loose (not fitted), thin cotton sweater
- ruler
- chalk
- scissors
- fusible bonding tape
- iron and ironing board
- snap pliers or setting tool
- decorative snaps with prongs
- cardboard
- stick-on stencils
- foam paintbrush
- fabric paint

What You'll Do

1. Use a ruler and chalk to draw a straight line down the front of your sweater all the way from the top to the bottom. Cut along the line through only the front of the sweater.

2. Fold in each cut side 1 inch (2.5 cm). Following the instructions on the package, use fusible bonding tape and an iron to create a hem.

3. On one side of the opening, mark a dot at the top. Then mark dots every 2 inches (5.1 cm) all the way down to the bottom. The dots should be about 0.5 inch (1.3 cm) in from the edge. Repeat for the other side of the opening. Make sure the dots line up on both sides.

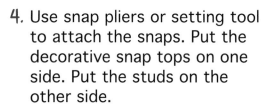

4. Use snap pliers or setting tool to attach the snaps. Put the decorative snap tops on one side. Put the studs on the other side.

5. Lay the cardigan flat on your workspace. Put a piece of cardboard inside. Stick on a stencil. Dab on fabric paint. Peel off the stencil. Let the paint dry completely.

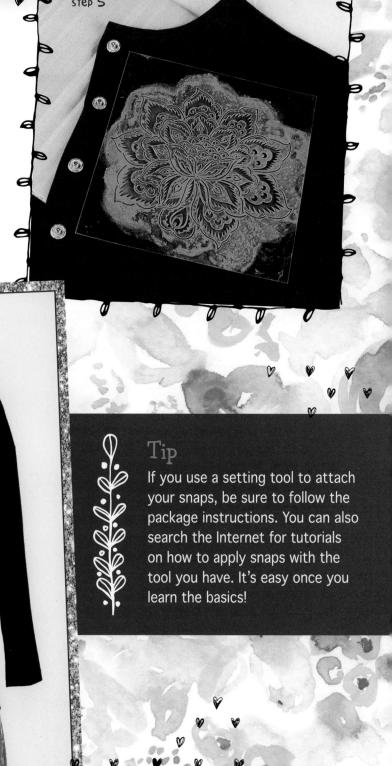

step 5

Tip

If you use a setting tool to attach your snaps, be sure to follow the package instructions. You can also search the Internet for tutorials on how to apply snaps with the tool you have. It's easy once you learn the basics!

Read More

Bolte, Mari. *Fab Fashions You Can Make and Share*. Sleepover Girls Crafts. North Mankato, Minn.: Capstone, 2015.

Rissman, Rebecca. *Fashion Hacks: Your Fashion Failures Solved!*. North Mankato, Minn.: Capstone, 2018.

Ware, Lesley. *How to Be a Fashion Designer*. New York: DK Publishing, 2018.

Internet Sites

Use FactHound to find Internet sites related to this book.

Visit *www.facthound.com*

Just type in 9781543525519 and go.